Rainforests

Kate Riggs

CREATIVE EDUCATION • CREATIVE PAPERBACKS

seedlings

Published by Creative Education and Creative Paperbacks
P.O. Box 227, Mankato, Minnesota 56002
Creative Education and Creative Paperbacks
are imprints of The Creative Company
www.thecreativecompany.us

Design by Ellen Huber; production by Joe Kahnke
Art direction by Rita Marshall
Printed in the United States of America

Photographs by Alamy (frans lemmens, Science Photo
Library), Corbis (Gerry Ellis/Minden Pictures), Dreamstime
(Hotshotsworldwide, Hpphoto, Ijacky, Isselee, Dennis Jacobsen,
Jaggat ..., Janossygergely, Iakov Kalinin, Koh Sze Kiat,
Lightpoet, Lisastrachan, Juriah Mosin, Mr.suchat Tepruang,
Puwanai Ponchai, Rungrote, Takepicsforfun, Tolotola,
Wichugorn Wattanakul), iStockphoto (malerapaso, MorelSO),
Shutterstock (iSiripong)

Library of Congress Cataloging-in-Publication Data
Riggs, Kate.
Rainforests / Kate Riggs.
p. cm. — (Seedlings)
Includes bibliographical references and index.
Summary: A kindergarten-level introduction to rainforests,
covering their climate, plant and animal life, and such
defining features as their tall trees.
ISBN 978-1-60818-744-7 (hardcover)
ISBN 978-1-62832-340-5 (pbk)
ISBN 978-1-56660-779-7 (eBook)
1. Rainforests—Juvenile literature. 2. Rainforest ecology—
Juvenile literature.
QH541.5.R27 R54 2016
577.34—dc23   2015041991
CCSS: RI.K.1, 2, 3, 4, 5, 6, 7;
RI.1.1, 2, 3, 4, 5, 6, 7; RF.K.1, 3; RF.1.1

First Edition HC 9 8 7 6 5 4 3 2 1
First Edition PBK 9 8 7 6 5 4 3 2 1

TABLE OF CONTENTS

Hello, Rainforest! **5**

Warm Rains **6**

All about Trees **8**

Rainforest Plants **11**

Animal Variety **12**

Canopy Heights **15**

Rainforest in Action **16**

Goodbye, Rainforest! **19**

Picture a Rainforest **20**

Words to Know **22**

Read More **23**

Websites **23**

Index **24**

Hello, rainforest!

Rainforests are places that get lots of rain. They are warm and wet.

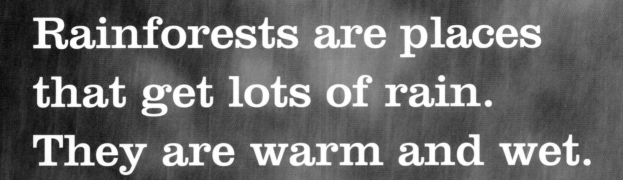

Tall trees grow in rainforests. Sloths hang from trees by their long claws.

Snakes curl around branches.

Some plants grow on trees. Others have big leaves that catch water. Fruits and nuts grow, too.

Monkeys swing through the forest. Sticky tree frogs grip plants.

Bugs fly and hide.

The tallest trees are about 200 feet tall. Other trees grow below them. They make up the canopy.

Rain falls in the
forest. It gathers
in plants.

Animals like coatis move up and down the trees.

Goodbye, rainforest!

Picture a Rainforest

emergent layer

canopy

three-toed sloth

understory

river

kapok tree

blue-and-yellow macaw

millipede

forest floor

21

Words to Know

canopy: the second-highest layer of a rainforest, with most of the tall trees

claws: curved nails on the toes of some animals

Read More

Heos, Bridget. *Do You Really Want to Visit a Rainforest?*
Mankato, Minn.: Amicus, 2015.

Riggs, Kate. *Monkeys.*
Mankato, Minn.: Creative Education, 2013.

Websites

Rainforest Alliance: Kids' Corner
http://www.rainforest-alliance.org/kids
Play games and do other activities to learn about rainforests.

Rainforest Rangers
http://therainforestrangers.com/
Help save the Costa Rican rainforest!

Note: Every effort has been made to ensure that the websites listed above are suitable for children, that they have educational value, and that they contain no inappropriate material. However, because of the nature of the Internet, it is impossible to guarantee that these sites will remain active indefinitely or that their contents will not be altered.

23

Index

bugs **13**
canopy **15**
coatis **17**
frogs **12**
monkeys **12**
plants **11, 12, 16**
rain **6, 16**
sloths **8**
snakes **9**
trees **8, 11, 15, 17**